BE YOUR
BEST
YOU

BE AWARE!

A HERO'S GUIDE TO
BEING SMART AND STAYING SAFE

ELSIE OLSON

Consulting Editor, Diane Craig, M.A./Reading Specialist

Super Sandcastle

An Imprint of Abdo Publishing
abdobooks.com

abdobooks.com

Published by Abdo Publishing, a division of ABDO, PO Box 398166, Minneapolis, Minnesota 55439. Copyright © 2020 by Abdo Consulting Group, Inc. International copyrights reserved in all countries. No part of this book may be reproduced in any form without written permission from the publisher. Super SandCastle™ is a trademark and logo of Abdo Publishing.

Printed in the United States of America, North Mankato, Minnesota
052019
092019

THIS BOOK CONTAINS
RECYCLED MATERIALS

Design: Sarah DeYoung, Mighty Media, Inc.
Production: Mighty Media, Inc.
Editor: Jessica Rusick
Cover Photographs: Shutterstock Images
Interior Photographs: iStockphoto; Mighty Media, Inc.; Shutterstock Images

Library of Congress Control Number: 2018966957

Publisher's Cataloging-in-Publication Data
Names: Olson, Elsie, author.
Title: Be aware!: a hero's guide to being smart and staying safe / by Elsie Olson
Other title: A hero's guide to being smart and staying safe
Description: Minneapolis, Minnesota : Abdo Publishing, 2020 | Series: Be your best you
Identifiers: ISBN 9781532119644 (lib. bdg.) | ISBN 9781532174407 (ebook)
Subjects: LCSH: Safety education--Juvenile literature. | Children and the Internet--Juvenile literature. |
    Playgrounds--Safety measures--Juvenile literature. | Schools--Safety measures--Juvenile literature. |
    Accidents--Prevention | Heroism--Juvenile literature.
Classification: DDC 613.6--dc23

Super SandCastle™ books are created by a team of professional educators, reading specialists, and content developers around five essential components—phonemic awareness, phonics, vocabulary, text comprehension, and fluency—to assist young readers as they develop reading skills and strategies and increase their general knowledge. All books are written, reviewed, and leveled for guided reading, early reading intervention, and Accelerated Reader™ programs for use in shared, guided, and independent reading and writing activities to support a balanced approach to literacy instruction.

CONTENTS

BE YOUR BEST YOU!

Do you look both ways before crossing the street? When you ride in a car, do you buckle your seat?

If someone says something that makes you feel bad, do you tell someone you trust, like your mom or your dad?

YOU HAVE THE POWER.
BE A HERO TOO.
BE SAFE AND AWARE.

BE YOUR BEST
YOU!

WHAT IS AWARENESS?

Being aware means paying attention. People who are aware watch. They listen too. This **information** helps them stay safe. It also helps them make healthy choices.

Are You Aware?

- Do you wear a helmet when riding a bike or skateboard?

- Do you tell an adult you trust if someone makes you feel **uncomfortable**?

- Do you protect your personal information online?

These are signs of awareness!

BE AWARE!

Being aware is more than watching and listening. It also means paying attention to how you feel. You might have a bad feeling about someone. Or you might trust someone. These feelings are your **instincts**.

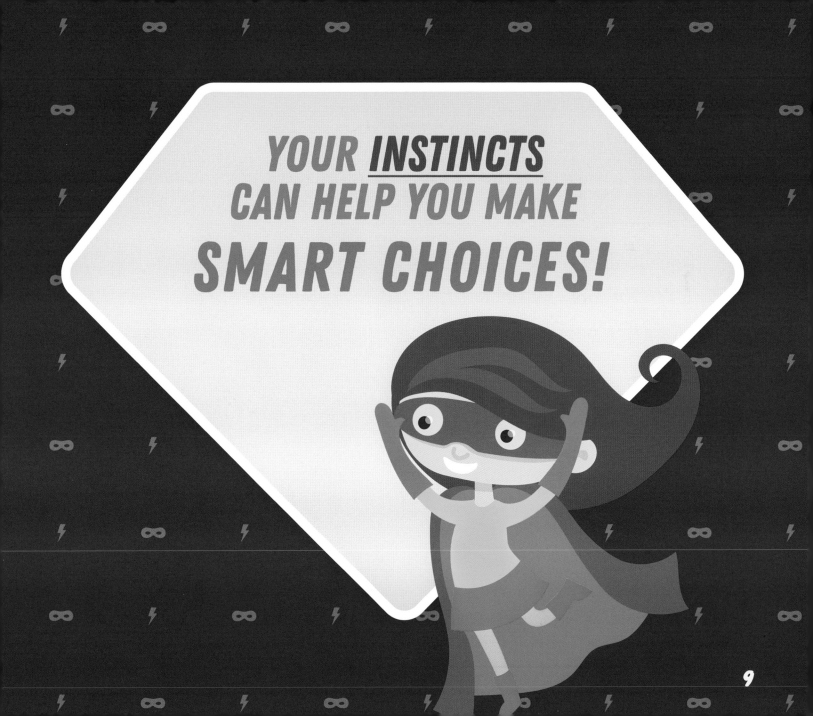

YOUR **INSTINCTS** CAN HELP YOU MAKE SMART CHOICES!

SUPERPOWER!
INSTINCTS

The world is a safe place for most kids. But some people harm kids. So it's good to stay aware.

10

YOUR **INSTINCTS** ARE LIKE A SUPERPOWER.

They can help you know if someone wants to hurt you. Does an adult make you **uncomfortable**? That's a sign they may be doing something wrong.

You don't have to be **polite** if this happens. Yell and scream. Get away from the person.

SMART SAFETY CHOICES

You have the power to make smart choices every day. These choices help protect your body!

FIVE SIMPLE SAFETY CHOICES

★ Look both ways before crossing a street.

★ Wear a helmet when riding on a toy with wheels.

★ Wear a seatbelt in the car.

★ Wear a life jacket on the water.

★ Dress for the weather.

SUPERPOWER!
BE TECH SMART

Many people use the internet. That means you need your tech smarts! These skills can keep you safe online.

SIX SUPER TECH RULES

★ Don't visit sites meant for older kids or adults.

★ Don't share your name, address, or phone number online.

★ Don't post photos of yourself online.

★ Don't share photos of others without their **permission**.

★ Only share passwords with your parents.

★ Tell an adult if someone posts something mean or scary.

JUST SAY NO

Your body is yours. Other people should not touch it without your **permission**. If someone tries to touch you, say no! Then tell an adult you trust right away.

HOW ABOUT A HIGH FIVE?

Sometimes people will want to hug or kiss you. It's okay if you don't want to. Ask if you can high five instead!

USE YOUR VOICE

Your voice is a great superpower. It can be loud when you need help. It can tell an adult when something scary is happening.

> So speak up if something feels wrong.

NO SECRETS!

Kids shouldn't keep secrets from their parents. If someone asks you to keep a secret, tell an adult you trust right away.

FIND A SUPER ADULT

Some problems are too big for kids to handle. That's why one superpower is finding an adult you can trust. Tell this person if you are ever worried or scared about something.

STRANGERS YOU CAN TRUST

Sometimes you might need help when your super adult isn't there. Use your **instinct** to find a stranger you can trust. Try:

A SECURITY GUARD OR PARK RANGER

A PARENT WITH CHILDREN

A STORE WORKER WITH A NAMETAG

BE A HERO!

It's your turn to take a
stand. Act like a hero.
Lend a hand.

With the words you say
and the things you do,
be aware and stay safe.
Be your best you!

22

WHAT WOULD YOU DO?

Being a hero is about making smart and safe choices. How would you use your superpowers in the situations below?

An adult you don't know offers to give you a ride home.

Someone posts a picture of you online without your **permission**.

A kid you don't know asks to borrow your phone.

GLOSSARY

information – the facts known about an event or subject.

instinct – a natural pattern of behavior that people are born with.

permission – when a person says it's okay to do something.

polite – having good manners or showing consideration for others. Someone who is polite shows politeness.

uncomfortable – bad or hurtful.

ONLINE RESOURCES

Booklinks
NONFICTION NETWORK
FREE! ONLINE NONFICTION RESOURCES

To learn more about being aware, smart, and safe, visit **abdobooklinks.com** or scan this QR code. These links are routinely monitored and updated to provide the most current information available.